Forces & Friction

Peter Riley

A^+

Smart Apple Media

This book has been published in cooperation with Franklin Watts.

Editor: Rachel Tonkin, Designer: Proof Books, Picture researcher: Diana Morris, Artwork: Ian Thompson

Picture credits:
Leslie Garland Picture Library/Alamy: 6t, 7b; Lowell Georgia/Corbis: 19c; Martin Harvey/Alamy: 12t; Joe McBride/Corbis: 23t; Model Images Ltd./Alamy: 15c; NASA: 11; Phototake Inc./Alamy: 12b; Reuters/Corbis: 14t; Alwyn J. Roberts/FLPA Images: 20t; Richard Hamilton Smith/Corbis: 17; Stockshot/Alamy: 1ot; Topfoto: 21t. 23t; Clive Tully/Alamy: 4; D.P.Wilson/FLPA Images: 18.

All other images: Andy Crawford

With thanks to our model: Gloria Maddy

Published in the United States by Smart Apple Media
2140 Howard Drive West, North Mankato, Minnesota 56003

Library of Congress Cataloging-in-Publication Data

Riley, Peter D.
Forces & friction / by Peter Riley.
p. cm. — (Essential science)
Includes index.
ISBN-13: 978-1-59920-026-2
1. Force and energy—Juvenile literature. 2. Friction—Juvenile literature. I. Title. II. Title: Forces and friction.

QC73.4.R488 2007
531—dc22   2006030983

9 8 7 6 5 4 3 2 1

CONTENTS

FORCES AND FRICTION

A force is a push or a pull. Close this book and then open it again. You used pushes to close it and pulls to open it. All kinds of movements come from pushes and pulls.

This dog is pulling on the leash.

What forces can do

A force can make something start to move, go faster or slower, change direction, or stop. Forces can change the shape of things by flattening, stretching, bending, or twisting them.

Many kinds of forces

You cannot see forces but you can see and feel their effects. A force that pulls on us all the time is the pull of gravity.

Gravity pulls us toward Earth. Another force is friction, which occurs when two surfaces rub together. When you ride your bicycle, you can feel a force called air resistance pushing against your face. If you try to walk in a swimming pool, you feel a force called water resistance slowing you down. One of the most fascinating forces is magnetism, which only pulls on iron and steel.

Scientists use arrows to show the direction and size of a force when you squeeze, stretch, bend, and twist something.

Pointing the way

Even though a force cannot be seen, scientists show where it is in a picture by drawing an arrow. The arrow shows the direction in which the force is pushing or pulling. The size of the arrow shows the size of the force.

Measuring a force

A force meter is used to measure a force. It measures the strength of the force in pounds or newtons (N). You can judge the strength of a small force if you remember that an average-sized apple pushes on your hand with a force of approximately 0.45 pounds or 2 newtons.

This force meter has a scale on it that measures force in units called newtons.

Use the data

When scientists do experiments, they make observations and record them. This information is called data. It may be recorded in a table, bar graph, or line graph. Collect some data about how paper falls to the ground by trying this activity. Take two pieces of paper. Crumple one up into a ball (A) and fold the other (B). Hold the two pieces at the same height and let them fall. Record which one reached the ground first. Repeat three times and record your results in a table like this one. How does your data compare? Answers to all of the questions in this book are on page 31.

Trial	A first	B first	same time
1	✓		
2	✓		
3	✓		
4	✓		

MAGNETS

Magnets have the power to pull certain kinds of metal objects toward them. Some magnets are made by using electricity and are called electromagnets.

Where does the name come from?

More than 2,000 years ago, a rock was found that made pieces of iron cling to it. It was discovered in a country called Magnesia, which is now part of Turkey. The rock was called magnetite after the place it was found. When metal bars were made that could attract iron, they were called magnets.

Magnetite is a rock that contains iron.

The arrow shows the magnetic force pulling on the paper clips.

Making a magnet

A small bar of iron or steel can be made into a magnet by stroking it with magnetite. Once a magnet is made, it can be used to make another magnet by stroking another bar of iron or steel with it.

Magnetic metals

A magnet does not pull all kinds of metal objects to it, just objects made from iron and steel. Other metals, such as aluminum, copper, and gold, are not pulled toward a magnet.

Uses of magnets

You probably have magnets on your refrigerator door. The magnet pulls on the steel in the refrigerator door to stay in place. The magnetic force is so strong that it can even pull through paper if you hold up a message with it. There is also a magnetic strip just inside the refrigerator door. It holds the door shut by pulling on the steel frame around it. When you open a refrigerator, you pull against the magnetic force.

Magnets are used for many things, such as keeping the refrigerator door shut.

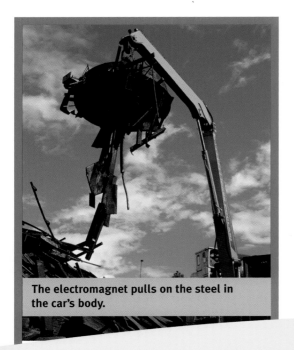

The electromagnet pulls on the steel in the car's body.

Electromagnets

An electromagnet is made by winding wire around a piece of iron. When electricity passes through the wire, the iron turns into a magnet. When the electricity is switched off, the iron loses its magnetism. Electromagnets have more uses than ordinary magnets. Very powerful electromagnets are used in scrap yards to move cars around. Some electromagnets can be quickly switched on and off. They are used in radio speakers, CD players, or TVs to make vibrations that we hear as sound.

Strength of magnets

This bar graph shows the strength of four magnets by how many paper clips they can hold.

1 How many more paper clips could D hold compared to C?

2 How many times stronger is B than A?

MAGNETIC POLES

The most powerful parts of a magnet are the poles. They are at each end of a magnet.

Earth's magnet

Scientists believe that there is iron at the center of Earth that acts like a huge magnet. One end of this magnet is near Earth's North Pole, and the other end is near Earth's South Pole.

North and South Poles

If a magnet is put on a piece of wood floating in a bowl of water, something special happens. The magnet turns so that one end points toward Earth's North Pole and the other end toward Earth's South Pole. The end pointing toward the North Pole is called the north-seeking pole, or north pole, of the magnet. The end pointing south is called the south-seeking, or south, pole of the magnet.

Pushing and pulling

If the north poles or south poles of two magnets are brought together, they push each other away. They are said to repel each other. If a north and south pole are brought together, they pull each other close. They are said to attract each other.

north

south

The magnet on the string moves toward the other magnet.

The magnetic field

The area around a magnet where its force acts is called the magnetic field. You can see it by using a bar magnet, plastic wrap, and iron shavings. Wrap the magnet in plastic wrap and put it on a piece of cardboard. Sprinkle iron shavings around it. The iron shavings make lines called lines of force. They are closest together near the ends of the magnet, which shows that the magnetic force is most powerful nearest the poles. The lines farther away from the magnet have larger distances between them. This means that the magnet's force is weaker at a distance from the magnet.

The iron shavings line up to show the magnetic field around this magnet.

Using a compass

A compass has a magnetic needle that can turn freely. One end points north and the other end south. Below the needle there is a card showing all directions, including east and west. You use a compass to find directions by lining up the needle with north and with south on the card.

A compass is used to find directions.

Repel or attract?

1 Which pairs of magnets are attracted to each other?

2 Which pairs of magnets repel each other?

A
N–N

B
N–S

C
S–S

D
S–N

GRAVITY AND WEIGHT

If you let go of an object, it falls to the ground. A force is pulling it down. We call this force gravity.

Where is the force of gravity?

There is a force of gravity between any two objects in the universe. The force of gravity acts from the center of each object. Most of these forces are very tiny and do not affect either of the objects. However, if one object is very large, its pull on another, smaller object can actually move it. Earth is a huge object compared to you, so its gravity never stops pulling on you.

Many people think that gravity just pulls you to Earth's surface, but actually the force pulls objects to the center of Earth. This is why objects fall down holes. If it were possible, they would keep falling until they reached Earth's center.

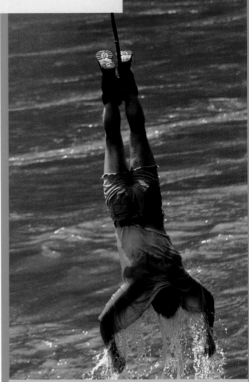

This bungee jumper was pulled down by the force of gravity acting between the center of his body and the center of Earth.

Weight

If an object is put on a force meter, the pull is measured in pounds or newtons. This force of gravity is called weight.

If you stand on one leg with your arms out, your muscles generate forces to stop the pull of gravity from making you fall over.

Why weight changes

If you were to take an object to the moon and weigh it on a force meter, you would find that the object had lost weight. It would be the same size because its mass (see below) had not changed. The reason for the weight loss is due to the gravity of the moon. The moon is a smaller object than Earth, so its gravity pulls less strongly on the objects close to it. The moon's gravity is six times weaker than Earth's gravity, so objects on the moon weigh six times less than they do on Earth.

People are six times lighter on the moon. This allows them to move or jump around more easily.

Mars is a smaller planet than Earth but is larger than the moon. Its gravity is three times less than that of Earth. Objects on Mars weigh three times less than they do on Earth.

Heavier or lighter?

The mass of an object is the amount of matter in it, and it is measured in kilograms (kg).

Here are the weights of three masses on Earth, Mars, and the moon.

1 How much does the weight of a one kilogram mass change when it moves from Earth to Mars?
2 How much does the weight of a two kilogram mass change when it moves from Earth to the moon?
3 How much does the weight of the three kilogram mass change from the moon to Earth?
4 Where would it be easiest to climb a steep hill, on Earth, Mars, or the moon?

EARTH	
Mass (kg)	Weight (lb)
1	2.2
2	4.5
3	6.7

MARS	
Mass (kg)	Weight (lb)
1	0.7
2	1.5
3	2.2

MOON	
Mass (kg)	Weight (lb)
1	0.37
2	0.75
3	

ELASTIC MATERIALS

When an elastic material is stretched then released, it springs back to its original length. This happens because of a force called tension.

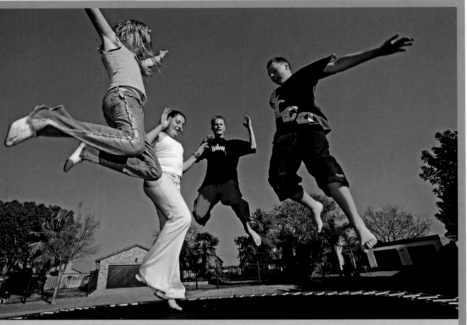

The tension in the elastic material in the trampoline pushes these children into the air.

Rubber, plastic, and metal

Rubber is an elastic material made from the juice of the rubber tree. Elastic plastics, which are made from chemicals in oil, look and act like rubber. Steel is a metal that has elastic properties when it is made into springs. You can read about springs on page 14.

Tension

When an elastic material is pulled, a force develops in it that pulls in the opposite direction. This force is a strain force called tension.

Pulling against the tension in these ropes helps to build up this athlete's muscles.

Releasing the tension

If the pull on a rubber band is slowly decreased, the rubber band slowly returns to its original shape. However, if the pull on the rubber band is suddenly removed, the rubber band moves very quickly—or snaps—back to its original shape. You can see tension in action on a trampoline. If you jump on a trampoline, your weight pushes down on the elastic material to create tension, which then pushes you back into the air. Similarly, in some toys you can stretch or twist rubber bands to create tension and make the toys move by letting go. If the tension in a rubber band cannot match the pulling force that is stretching it, the rubber band snaps.

Using the tension

The wood of some trees has elastic properties and has been used to make bows for centuries. When the tension is suddenly released in a bow, it provides the force needed to fire an arrow into the air. The tension in rubber bands is also used for more peaceful purposes, such as holding a bundle of letters together.

A tension force develops when a rubber band is twisted. It can be used to spin an airplane propeller and make the airplane go forward.

Stretching elastic

A rubber band had weights added to it. After each weight was added, the length of the rubber band was measured.

1 How much does a weight of 1 pound (0.5 kg) stretch the rubber band?

2 What happens to the length of the rubber band as the weight pulling on it increases?

3 What do you think might be the length of the rubber band if a weight of 5 pounds (2.3 kg) was attached to it?

4 What might happen to the rubber band if a weight of 55 pounds (25 kg) was attached to it?

Pounds (kg)	Length inches (cm)
0 (0)	3.9 (10)
1 (0.5)	4.3 (11)
2 (0.9)	4.7 (12)
3 (1.3)	5.1 (13)
4 (1.8)	5.5 (14)

SPRINGS

Springs are made from a metal wire that has been made into a coil. There are three kinds of springs: close-coil springs, open-coil springs, and spiral springs.

The weight of this sleeper makes the close-coil springs stretch, but the tension in the springs holds him off the ground.

Close-coil spring

In a close-coil spring, the coils touch each other. This means that the spring can only be stretched. When a close-coil spring is pulled, a tension force develops in the coils of metal to match it. When the pulling force is removed from the spring, the strain force makes it return to its original length.

The force meter

A force meter has a close-coil spring. At one end of the force meter, there is a hook for attaching a weight or for connecting to objects to be pulled. When the spring is stretched, a pointer on the spring moves down the scale. The strength of the force on the spring is shown by the position of the pointer when it stops moving. There are force meters with small springs for measuring small forces and large springs for measuring large forces.

Overstretching

If a close-coil spring is pulled too hard, it overstretches. When this happens, changes take place in the metal that stop the tension force from pulling it back to its original length. The spring then stays at its new, longer length. The metal or plastic body of a force meter stops the spring inside from overstretching.

Open-coil spring

In an open-coil spring, there are gaps between the coils. The gaps allow the spring to be flattened. When the spring is pushed down or flattened, a strain force called compression develops in the coils of metal to match it. When the flattening force is removed from the spring, the compression force makes the spring return to its original length.

If you squeeze an open-coiled spring between your fingers, the force in the spring pushes back. This force is called compression.

Spiral spring

A spiral spring is made from a strip of metal that has been wound up into a spiral. As the strip is wound up, a tension force develops inside. When the spring is fully wound, it has a very large tension force inside it. This can then be used to unwind the spring in a clockwork device. If the spring is attached to the wheels of a toy car, the tension force can push on them and make them turn.

When you wind up this robot, the tension force created makes it move.

Extending springs

A number of weights were added to a spring in turn. Each time a weight was added, the increase in length of the spring was recorded in a line graph.

1 How much did the spring extend when a weight of one pound (5 N) was attached?
2 How much would the spring extend when a weight of four pounds (20 N) was attached?
3 What weight would make the spring extend to 0.4 inches (10 mm) long?

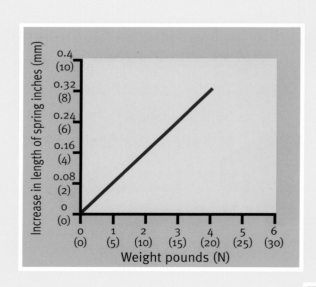

FRICTION

Friction is a force that develops when two surfaces are in contact with each other and one is pushed or pulled over the other one.

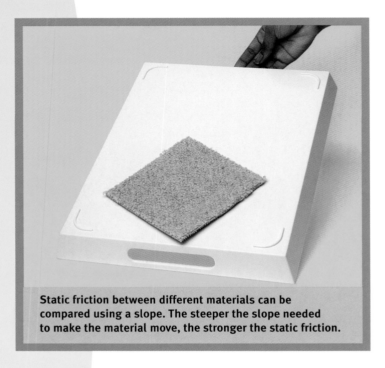

Static friction between different materials can be compared using a slope. The steeper the slope needed to make the material move, the stronger the static friction.

Two kinds of friction

There are two kinds of friction. They are called static and sliding friction. If you close this book, put it on a table, and very gently push it, it will not move. This is because static friction is pushing against you and holding the book in place. If you push a little more strongly, the book will start to move, but it will not whiz away across the table. It will move slowly because sliding friction is now pushing against you.

Measuring friction

You can measure both kinds of friction with a force meter. If you attach a force meter to a sneaker and very gently pull it, the sneaker will stay in place, but a force will be recorded on the meter's scale. If you pull harder, the sneaker will start to move, and you will see the pointer move farther back up the scale. This shows that sliding friction is weaker than static friction.

The grip of a sneaker is being measured by a force meter.

Rough and smooth surfaces

When something moves over a rough surface, a strong force of friction pushes on it. If something moves over a smooth surface, a weaker force of friction pushes on it. You can easily feel this by gently rubbing your finger over the cloth in your sleeve and then over this page. You need to push a little harder to move your finger on your sleeve because of greater friction—the surface of your sleeve is rougher than the surface of this page.

Increasing friction

Friction can be increased if you press two surfaces together. When you put the brakes on when riding a bicycle, the brake pads press against the rim of the wheel, which makes friction increase so much that it soon stops the bike from moving.

Reducing friction

People slip and slide on a wet floor but not on a dry one because friction helps their shoes to grip the floor. But when the floor is wet, its surface is smoother. This means there is less friction and less grip. Oil is used in machines, such as car engines, to reduce friction between the moving parts.

People slide on ice because there is little friction to stop them from moving.

Braking distance

Cars have brake pads that press against their wheels to make them stop. The table shows the distance needed to make a car stop when it is traveling at different speeds on a dry road.

Speed miles/hour (km/h)	Braking distance yards (m)
30 (48)	25 (23)
50 (80)	58 (53)
70 (112)	105 (96)

1 How does braking distance change as a car goes faster?

2 A car decreases its speed from 70 miles (112 km) per hour to 50 miles (80 km) per hour. How does its braking distance change?

3 How do you think the braking distances may change if the car was driven in wet weather?

WATER RESISTANCE

It's hard work to walk through the water in a swimming pool. As you move forward, you push on the water, but the force of water pushes back on you. This force is called water resistance.

The effect of shape

If you tried to walk through water carrying a suitcase in front of you, you would find it even harder to move. The suitcase has a large, flat surface. When you move the suitcase through water, the water cannot flow over it easily, so it piles up in front of the suitcase and pushes even harder. This makes the water resistance very high.

These fish have a streamlined shape, so water flows over them easily and allows them to move quickly through the water.

When a shape with a curved surface pushes through the water, the water resistance is lower. The water flows easily over the curves and does not pile up and push with a strong force. If the shape is pointed at the front and back like some fish, the water flows over it even more easily. A shape that reduces water resistance is called a streamlined shape.

Testing shapes

You can test different shapes to see if they are streamlined using modeling clay. Make the clay into different shapes and drop them into a tall cylinder of water. Measure the time it takes for them to reach the bottom. The most streamlined shape will fall the fastest, and the least streamlined shape will fall the slowest.

The modeling clay must be dropped from the same height for each test.

Boats

Water resistance acts at the surface of the water, too. If a boat has a hull that is pointed at the front, water will pass under it easily, and the boat will be able to move quickly. On the other hand, water would push hard on a boat with a flat front and make it move slowly.

The hull of a speed boat is streamlined, so there is very little water resistance to slow it down.

How do they fall?

The force of gravity pulls each shape down through the water, and at the same time, water resistance pushes up on it. Draw these shapes in order of falling (fastest first) from left to right. Draw an arrow showing the size of the water resistance on each one.

A

B

C

D

AIR RESISTANCE

Air resistance is a force that pushes on objects as they move through the air. It increases in size as the object moves faster.

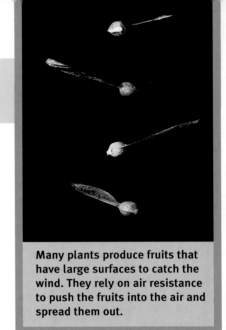

Many plants produce fruits that have large surfaces to catch the wind. They rely on air resistance to push the fruits into the air and spread them out.

Feeling air resistance

As you walk along, you cannot feel air resistance because it pushes with a very small force on your skin. When you get on your bike and begin to pedal, you move faster and faster and your face feels the push of the air more strongly.

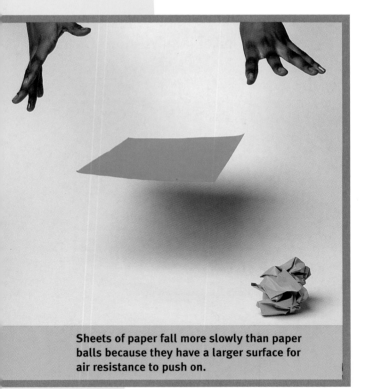

Sheets of paper fall more slowly than paper balls because they have a larger surface for air resistance to push on.

The size of surfaces

If you put a closed umbrella over your shoulder and ran with it, you could run quite fast. If you opened the umbrella and ran again, you would slow down. This is due to the size of the umbrella's surface moving through the air. When the umbrella is closed, there is only a small surface for the air to push on, so the air resistance is small. When the umbrella is open, there is a much larger surface for the air to push on, and the air resistance is high.

Wind and air resistance

You can feel air resistance when the wind blows, even if you are standing still. This is because of the speed of the air. Wind moves very fast, and the faster it moves, the harder it pushes. If you fly a kite in the wind, you can feel the air resistance pushing on the kite, and you have to pull hard on the string to keep it in place.

Air resistance and cars

When you run against the wind, you will find it is hard work. You will use up lots of energy pushing against the air resistance. Cars move quickly through the air, so their air resistance is high. They use up lots of energy in the form of gasoline. Cars are designed to be wedge shaped so that air flows over them more easily and reduces air resistance. This makes it easier for cars to move through the air so that they use less gasoline and make fewer exhaust gases, which cause pollution.

Falling through the air

When an object falls through the air, the air pushes on it. If the object has a small surface, such as a marble, the air resistance is low and the object falls fast. If the object has a large surface, such as a parachute, air resistance is higher and the object falls more slowly.

The air resistance on this parachute slows down the skydiver's fall so that he can land safely.

Which falls more quickly?

Make three squares of cloth into parachutes by tying one end of a piece of string to each corner then joining the other ends together and sticking them to a ball of modeling clay. The length of the sides of the cloth should be:

A = 2.5 inches (6 cm); B = 1.5 inches (4 cm);
C = 3 inches (8 cm).

1 Which cloth made the slowest-falling parachute?
2 Which cloth made the fastest-falling parachute?
3 What did you have to think about to find the answer?

BUOYANCY

Why do some things float and some things sink?
It all depends on a force called buoyancy.

Feel the buoyancy

Buoyancy is a force produced by water when an object is put in it. The object pushes some of the water out of the way to make space for itself. The water that has been pushed out of the way pushes back on the object with a force called buoyancy. Put your hand in a sink full of water and hold it steady. You can feel the water pushing on your skin. This push is the buoyancy.

Discovering buoyancy

Scientists found out about buoyancy in the following way. They placed an object on a force meter and measured its weight. Then they put the object in water while still attached to the force meter and made a discovery. The object weighed less in water than it did in air!

A special can with a spout on it was filled with water, and the object was put in it. The water that was pushed out of the way poured out of the spout. When the scientists weighed the water, they found that it had the same weight that the object had lost. This means that when an object is put in water, the water that is pushed away pushes back with a force that is the same as its weight. This pushing force is the buoyancy.

force meter

displacement can

object

water

spout

beaker

balance

This is the equipment that is used to measure the buoyancy.

This wooden boat floats on the water because it weighs less than the force pushing against it.

This cannon from an ancient boat sank because its weight was greater than the buoyancy pushing on it.

Floating and sinking

An object will float or sink depending on its weight and how much buoyancy is pushing on it. If an object weighs less than the buoyancy, it floats. If it weighs more than the buoyancy, it sinks. A big, heavy boat will float because its weight is distributed over a large surface area, so the buoyancy is large.

Did they float or sink?

Here are the weights of five objects and the buoyancy pushing on each of them.

1 Which objects floated?
2 Which objects sank?

Try doing this experiment on your own with things such as a pencil or a pebble.

Object	Weight pounds (N)	Buoyancy pounds (N)
A	2 (10)	1 (5)
B	3 (15)	4 (20)
C	2.7 (12)	0.9 (4)
D	1.6 (7)	2 (10)
E	1.8 (8)	1.3 (6)

BALANCED FORCES

When we study forces, we often look
at the effect of one force at a time.
It is important to remember that two
or more forces may be pushing and
pulling on an object at the same time.

Hanging around

An apple hanging from a force meter has two forces
pulling on it. The tension in the force meter pulls the apple
up, and the apple's weight, due to the pull of gravity, pulls
it down. Fruits on trees are held in place by the same two
forces; the tension is in the wood on the tree's twigs.

When a spring is squeezed

If you squeeze an open-coiled spring, two
pushing forces act against each other.
The fingers push down on the spring, and
the compression force in the spring
pushes it up.

The pull on a paper clip

If a paper clip is brought to one end
of a magnet and released, it will
hang there. The magnetic force of
the magnet pulls it up, and its weight
due to gravity pulls it down.

Stopping a slip

If you push against a box a little and the box stays in place, two forces are acting on it. You may think your pushing force is the only one at work, but underneath the box the force of static friction is holding it in place.

Floating

A wooden boat floating in water has two forces acting on it. Its weight due to gravity pulls it down, and buoyancy pushes it up.

Balanced forces

When you look at the arrows on each picture, you can see that they point in opposite directions. They are also the same size. This means that the size of one force acting in one direction is matched by the size of the force acting in the other direction. The two forces are equal, so the objects do not move.

Balancing the force

1 If an apple with a weight of 0.45 pounds (2 N) hangs from a twig, what is the size of the tension force in the twig?

2 If a steel object with a weight of 0.2 pounds (1 N) hangs from a magnet, what is the strength of the magnetic force holding it in place?

3 If a model boat with a weight of five pounds (25 N) floats on a pond, how much buoyancy is pushing against it?

UNBALANCED FORCES

Unbalanced forces can make a stationary object move and a moving object speed up, change direction, or slow down.

A falling apple

We saw on page 24 that an apple hanging from a force meter has two forces acting on it. The forces are the same size and pull in opposite directions. If the spring in the force meter was cut, the tension force would no longer pull upward on the apple. The pull of the apple's weight would not have a force to balance it, so the apple would fall, pulled down by gravity.

The weight of the parachute is greater than the air resistance pushing up, so the parachute falls.

Making a move

Boxes slide, parachutes fall, and empty bottles pop up to the water surface when the forces acting on them are unbalanced.

The pushing force on the box is stronger than the friction between the box and the surface, so the box moves.

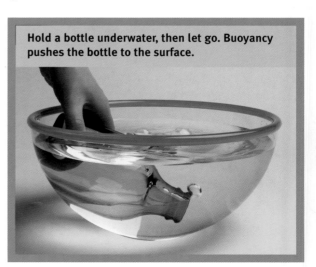

Hold a bottle underwater, then let go. Buoyancy pushes the bottle to the surface.

Riding a bicycle

If you sit on the seat of a bicycle and do not move, two balanced forces are acting on you and the bicycle. Your weight is pushing down, and the contact force with the ground is pushing up.

When you start to pedal, three other forces begin to act on you. There is the driving force made by your muscles, which moves you and the bicycle forward. There is air resistance, which pushes on you and the bicycle, and there is friction, which pushes on the bicycle tires where the tires touch the road.

At first, the air resistance is low, but as you move faster and faster, it rises until it matches your driving force. When this happens, you move along at a steady speed in a straight line.

If you turn the handlebars, the force made by your arm muscles makes the bicycle move in a new direction.

When any object is on the move, it tends to keep moving, even when there is no longer a force driving it along. This means that if you stop pedaling, you will still keep moving forward. However, the forces of air resistance and friction still push on you, and because they are not balanced by a driving force, you eventually stop.

You can stop even sooner if you put on the brakes (see page 17).

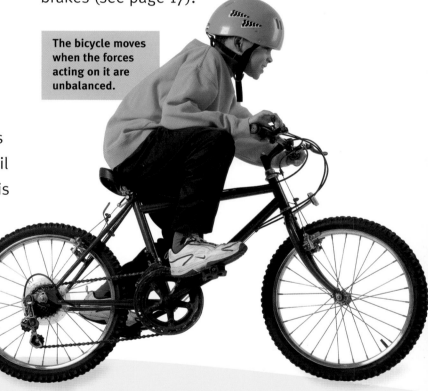

The bicycle moves when the forces acting on it are unbalanced.

Balanced or unbalanced forces

The table shows some forces acting on four objects.

1 Which objects are stationary?
2 Which objects are moving?

Object	Force pounds (N)	Force pounds (N)
A	weight 2 (10)	magnetic 2 (10)
B	weight 2 (10)	air resistance 1 (5)
C	friction 3 (15)	pushing force 3 (15)
D	weight 4 (20)	buoyancy 1.3 (6)

CAN YOU REMEMBER THE ESSENTIALS?

Here are the essential science facts about forces and friction. They are presented in the order you read about them in the book. Spend a couple of minutes learning each set of facts. If you can learn them all, you know all of the essentials about the forces around you.

Magnets (pages 6-7)

A magnet can be made from a bar of iron or steel.
An electromagnet is made by winding wire around a piece of iron and letting a current of electricity pass through the wire.
A magnet or electromagnet pulls on objects made of iron or steel.

Gravity and weight (pages 10-11)

There is a force of gravity between any two objects in the universe.
Earth's gravity pulls everything toward its center.
The pulling force on an object due to gravity is called its weight.

Magnetic poles (pages 8-9)

The magnetic poles are at each end of a magnet.
The two poles of a magnet are the north pole and south pole.
Opposite magnetic poles attract each other.
Similar magnetic poles repel each other.

Elastic materials (pages 12-13)

Elastic materials can be stretched but can spring back to their original shape.
The force that develops in an elastic material when it is stretched is called tension.
Rubber is an elastic material.

Springs (pages 14-15)

Springs are made from
a coil of wire.
Close-coil springs can be
stretched to create tension.
A force meter has a
close-coil spring in it.
Open-coil springs can
be squeezed.
The force that develops
in a squeezed spring is
called a compression force.
A spiral spring is used in
a clockwork device.

Friction (pages 16-17)

Friction develops when two surfaces rub
against each other. There are two different types
of friction: static friction and sliding friction.
A strong force of friction develops between
rough surfaces. A weak force of friction develops
between smooth surfaces.
Friction can be increased by pushing the surfaces
together.
Oil and water reduce friction.

Water resistance
(pages 18-19)

Water resistance is a force that
pushes on objects moving
through water.
Water resistance is also a force
that pushes on objects moving
across the water's surface.
An object with a streamlined
shape can move
quickly through
water or across
its surface.

Air resistance (pages 20-21)

Air resistance is a
force that pushes on
objects as they move
through the air.
As an object moves
faster, the air
resistance becomes
stronger. A large
surface area creates
more air resistance.

Buoyancy (pages 22-23)

Buoyancy is a force exerted by water
on an object put into it.
The buoyancy is the same as the
weight of water displaced by an
object in it. If the buoyancy is
greater than the object's
weight, the object floats.
If the buoyancy is less
than the object's weight,
the object sinks.

Balanced forces
(pages 24-25)

Two or more forces may be
pushing or pulling on
an object at the
same time.
If two forces are the
same size and push or
pull in opposite directions,
they are called balanced forces.

Unbalanced forces (pages 26-27)

Unbalanced forces make a stationary object move.

Unbalanced forces
make a moving
object speed up,
change direction,
or slow down.

GLOSSARY

Air resistance The push of the air on an object as the object moves forward.

Balance A device for weighing things.

Brake A device on a vehicle for slowing down the speed at which it travels.

Buoyancy The force of a liquid pushing upward on an object that has entered it.

Compass An instrument that uses a magnet to find directions.

Elastic A material that can spring back to its original shape after it has been stretched or twisted.

Electromagnet A device made from a length of wire coiled around a piece of iron. When electricity passes through the coil, the iron becomes a magnet.

Energy Something that allows an object or a living thing to take part in an activity such as moving or giving off light.

Exhaust gases The gases released from the exhaust pipe of a motor vehicle, such as a car.

Force meter An instrument for measuring forces. It has a scale that measures forces in pounds or newtons.

Friction A force that acts when two surfaces are in contact and one is pushed over the other. It acts in the opposite direction to the pushing force.

Gasoline A fuel made from oil that is used in car engines to provide energy for movement.

Gravity A force of attraction that exists between any two objects in the universe but only causes movement when one object is very much larger than the other.

Hull The part of a boat that rests in the water and supports other parts of the boat.

Iron shavings Tiny pieces of iron.

Lines of force Lines that show the strength of the magnetic force in different areas around a magnet.

Magnetic field The area around a magnet in which the magnetic force acts on magnetic materials.

Magnetism The force produced by a magnetic field or the effect of a magnet on magnetic objects.

Mass The amount of matter in an object.

Metal A substance with a shiny surface that conducts both heat and electricity well.

Muscles Tissues in the body that allow the parts of the body to move.

Plastic A solid material made from oil that does not conduct electricity but that can burn or melt easily.

Pollution Substances that are released into the environment and do not form a natural part of it. Pollution can harm living things.

Streamlined shape The shape of an object that allows air or water to easily flow over it and offers little resistance to the movement of the object.

Tension A force that is generated by an object when it is stretched.

Water resistance The push of the water on an object as the object moves forward through it.

Weight The force of an object pressing down toward the center of Earth as a result of gravity.

ANSWERS

Magnets (pages 6–7)

1 2.
2 Four times.

Magnetic Poles (pages 8–9)

1 B and D.
2 A and C.

Gravity and Weight (pages 10–11)

1 It is reduced by 1.5 pounds.
2 It is reduced by 3.75 pounds.
3 It increases by 5.6 pounds.
4 On the moon.

Elastic Materials (pages 12–13)

1 4.3 inches (11 cm).
2 It gets longer.
3 Increases to 5.9 inches (15 cm).
4 It might snap.

Springs (pages 14–15)

1 0.08 inches (2 mm).
2 0.32 inches (8 mm).
3 5 pounds (25 N).

Friction (pages 16–17)

1 It increases.
2 Decreases by 47 yards (43 m).
3 They would be longer because water reduces friction.

Water Resistance (pages 18–19)

A, B, D, C.
A would have the smallest arrow and C the largest.

Air Resistance (pages 20–21)

1 C.
2 B.
3 The size of the cloth.

Buoyancy (pages 22–23)

1 B and D.
2 A, C, and E.

Balanced Forces (pages 24–25)

1 0.45 pounds (2 N).
2 0.2 pounds (1 N).
3 5 pounds (25 N).

Unbalanced Forces (pages 26–27)

1 A and C.
2 B and D.

INDEX